First published in the USA in 2025 by Welbeck Children's Books
An imprint of Hachette Children's Group

Text for this edition adapted by Hannah Dolan

ISBN: 9781 80453 838 8

Writer: Simon Mugford
Designer and Illustrator: Dan Green
Designer: Arvind Shah
Design Manager: Sam James
Senior Commissioning Editor: Suhel Ahmed
Production: Melanie Robertson

Printed in China
10 9 8 7 6 5 4 3 2 1

Welbeck Children's Books
An imprint of Hachette Children's Group
Part of Hodder & Stoughton Limited
Carmelite House, 50 Victoria Embankment
London EC4Y 0DZ

SOCCER STORIES

SIMON MUGFORD

DAN GREEN

Meet one of the best soccer players in the world, Mo Salah.

SALAH! SALAH!

This Egyptian superstar with the huge smile has millions of fans in Africa and across the world.

What makes him awesome? Well, he's super quick and fantastic at dribbling.

When he shoots he almost always hits his target—so he scores lots and lots of goals!

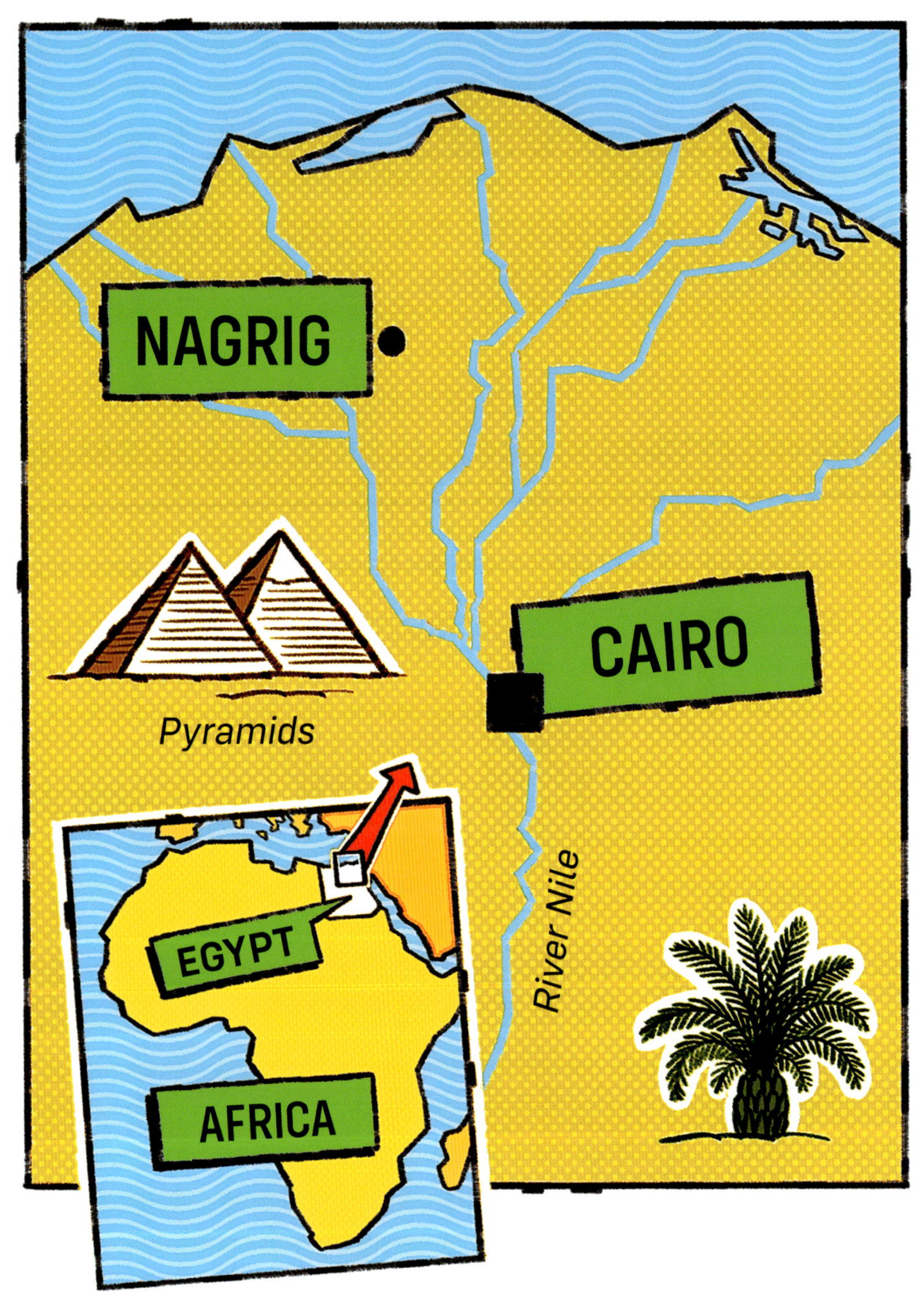

Mo was born in 1992 in a small farming village in Egypt called Nagrig. His full name is Mohamed Salah Hamed Mahrous Ghaly.

Little Mohamed lived in Nagrig with his mom and dad, and his younger brother, Nasr.

Mo always had a big smile and a big heart. As a boy, he would feed the stray dogs in Nagrig.

There was one thing that Mo and his brother Nasr loved more than anything else...playing soccer!
They played all the time on a dry, dusty soccer field in the center of Nagrig. They played there with other children from the village.

When Mo had the ball,
nobody could catch him—
not even the bigger boys!

Mo started playing for a local youth team called Ittihad Basyoun when he was 12.

He also saw a lot of soccer on TV with his friends in a café. He watched matches from the Champions League—the competition featuring the top soccer clubs in Europe.

Ryan Giggs
Francesco Totti
Mo dreamed about being a superstar player. His heroes were Zinedine Zidane, Ronaldo Nazario, Ryan Giggs, and Francesco Totti.

One day, a man named Reda El-Mallah came to Nagrig. He was a soccer scout—his job was to find talented new players.

Reda came to watch a boy called Sherif play in a match with Mo and other boys in Nagrig. Sherif was good...

...but Mo was better!

WHO IS **THAT** KID?
It was on that day that Mo's journey to becoming a soccer star had begun.

When he was 14, Mo joined the youth team at El Mokawloon, one of the top teams in Egypt. El Mokawloon was in the Egyptian capital city of Cairo, a long way from Mo's home.

To train with the club in Cairo, Mo had to travel by bus for more than four hours. The buses were small, hot, and crowded. Some of the roads were bumpy and dangerous.

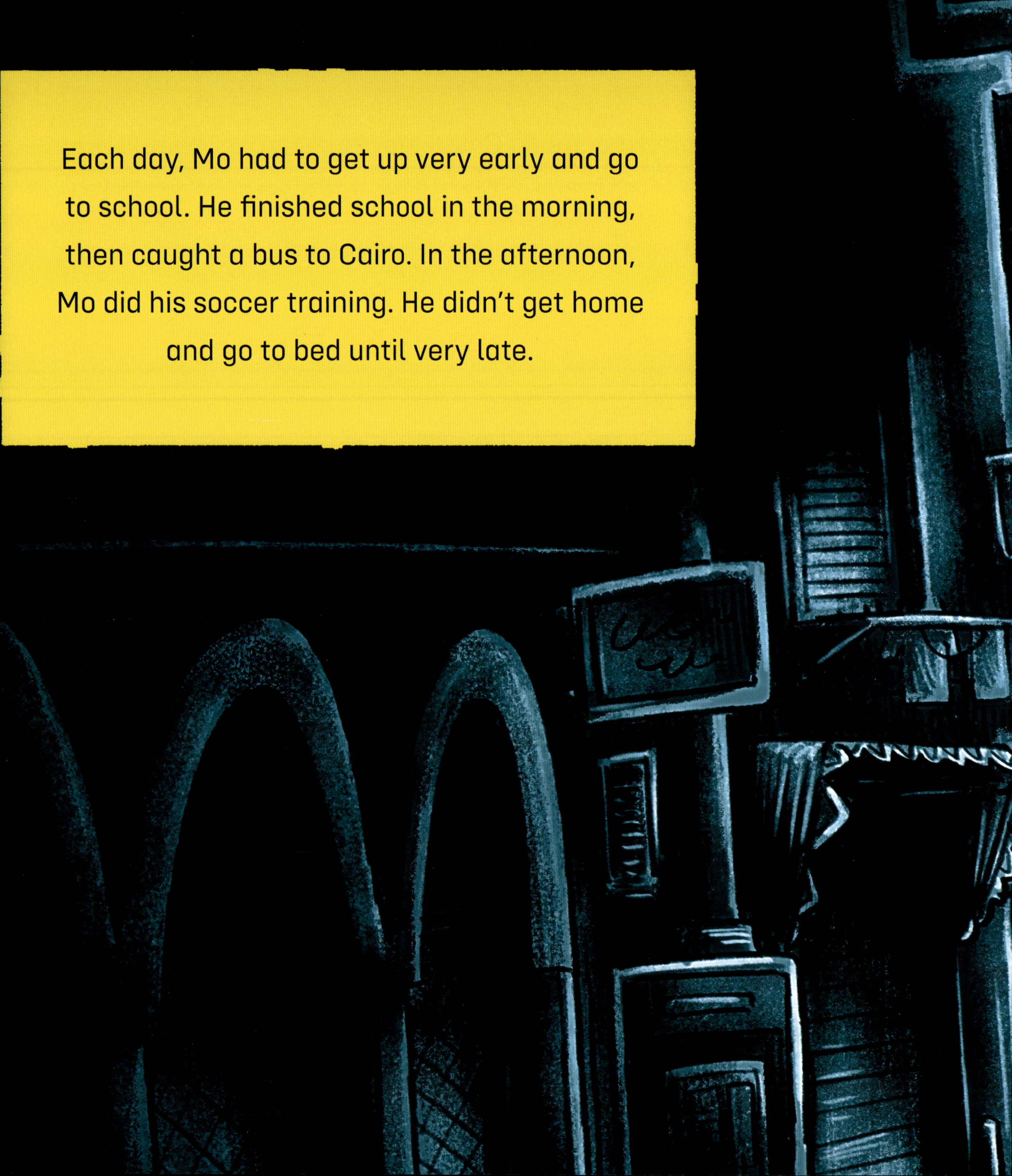

Each day, Mo had to get up very early and go to school. He finished school in the morning, then caught a bus to Cairo. In the afternoon, Mo did his soccer training. He didn't get home and go to bed until very late.

Mo's busy days left him very tired, but he really wanted to become a star like his heroes. He knew that all the hard work would be worth it.

On the El Mokawloon youth team, Mo started playing as a left back. This means he was a defender on the left side of the field. But he was not happy. He really wanted to score goals.

Mo's coaches saw how unhappy he was and moved him to the right wing. He then scored 34 goals in one season! Mo was smiling again.

When Mo was 18, he started playing for El Mokawloon's first team. The club also signed another player named Mo. Mo Elneny was the same age, and the two Mos became great friends.

Mo started to shine and score goals at El Mokawloon, and he began to play for Egypt too.

He traveled to Colombia in South America to play in the Under-20 World Cup.

Then Mo played for Egypt in the 2012 Olympic Games in London. He scored three goals—one in each of Egypt's games.
LONDON 2012

In 2017, Mo scored twice in a qualifying match against Congo to help Egypt reach the World Cup finals for the first time in many years.

The crowd and the whole of Egypt went wild. Mo was a national hero!

Back in 2012, Mo was the most exciting player in Egypt and the country's biggest clubs wanted to sign him. But Mo wanted to play in Europe, so he decided to play for Basel—one of the best clubs in Switzerland.

Switzerland was very different from Egypt. Mo had to learn a new language and make new friends. But things got easier when Mo's friend Mo Elneny started playing for Basel, too!

In 2013, Basel made it into the Champions League and they played against the English club Chelsea. In two games, Mo scored two goals against Chelsea.

Chelsea's manager, Jose Mourinho, decided to sign Mo. But at Chelsea, Mo struggled to score goals and Mourinho picked other players before him.

Chelsea sent Mo to play for two different clubs in Italy —Fiorentina in Florence, then AS Roma in Rome.

Mo played brilliantly in Italy, and in 2017 he signed for one of the biggest clubs in England: Liverpool.

Mo had an incredible first season and the team made it to the Champions League final. But Mo got injured during the match and Liverpool lost the game.

Then in Mo's next season, Liverpool reached the final again...and this time, they won! They were the champions of Europe.

Mo helped Liverpool to win
the Premier League in 2020.
They were English champions
for the first time in 30 years.

Mo has become one of the most famous people on the planet.
There is even a mural of him in New York City.

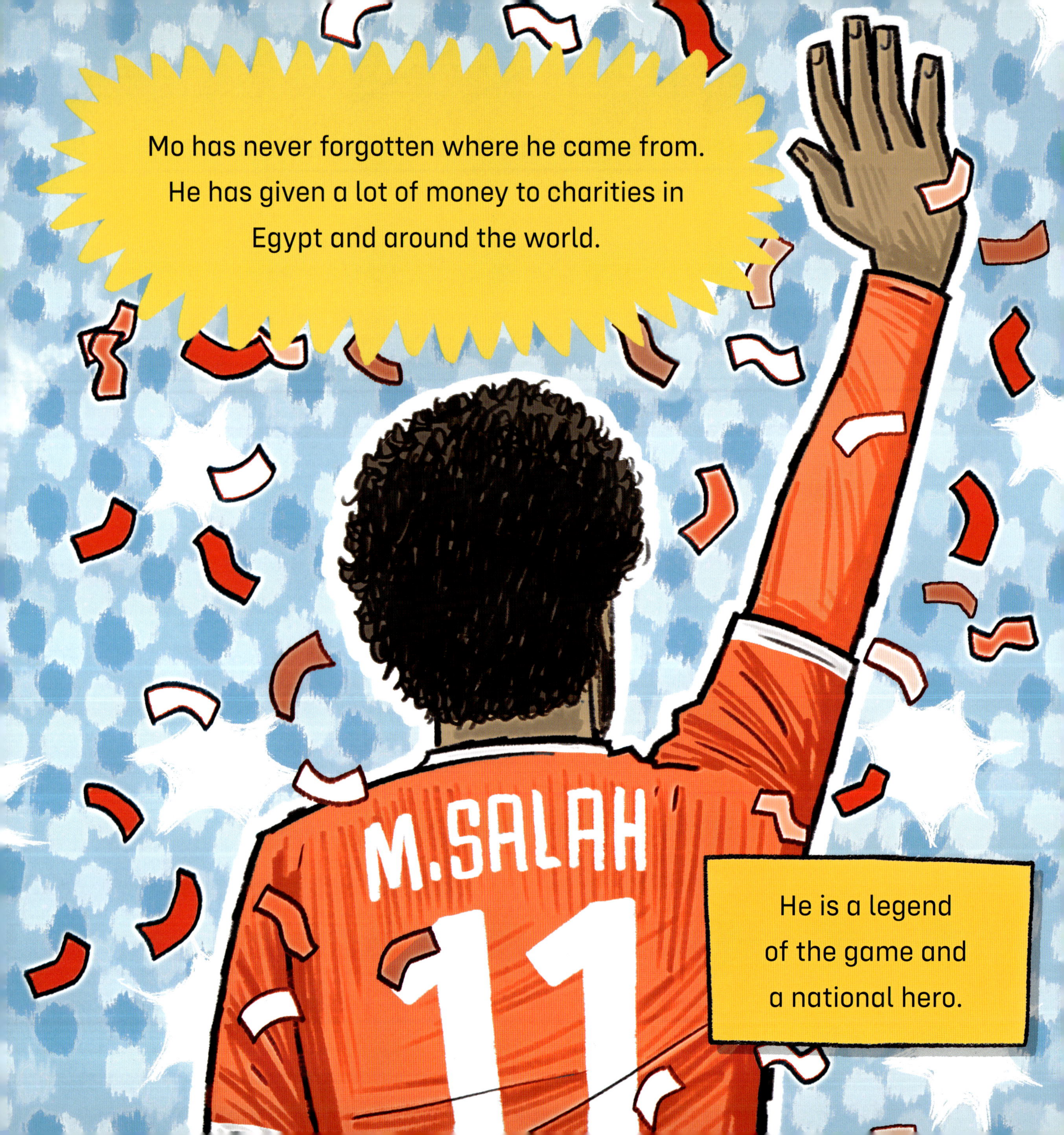

Mo has never forgotten where he came from. He has given a lot of money to charities in Egypt and around the world.

He is a legend of the game and a national hero.